HEAVEN ON EARTH

The power in healing and becoming the woman God has called you to be

IRENE BARRERA

Heaven on Earth copyright ©2022 by Irene Barrera
Published by Serene Purpose
ISBN: 978-0-578-39911-9

Contents

This book is dedicated to all you beautiful souls facing heartbreak, or currently in a relationship that causes you more pain than joy, but you simply don't know how to let go because you are scared of the unknown - and although you know what's best, you just don't know how.

My prayer to you is that you let go and trust God... through Him you will find everything you've been searching for. I pray that you find healing, purpose, and peace. You are worthy of the life you desire.

Preface: My Story

This book was prophesied on my life on June 10, 2017. At the time, I had no clue what it looked like. All I remember was Pastor Ivette Monge declaring, "A new season is to come. You have something very special; you will bring Heaven on earth."

I felt compelled to start writing in 2018. I was going through a very dark season in an unhealthy relationship not blessed by God. At the time I started writing, I was going through a breakup with this person. I got closer to God during this season: I removed every distraction, and started praying more. I went to church every service there was, and gave up worldly things to build a stronger relationship with God, and I started writing.

I had no idea this would turn out to be *Heaven on Earth;* the words that were declared on my life by this prophet were in the form of a book. At the time I started writing, I knew God wanted me to write about what I was experiencing in hopes of helping me to heal, encourage, and empower women in a similar situation. It was the way I had been releasing all that I was going through, sharing God's insights as I received them and allowing Him to guide me. I expected it to become a book at some point, but didn't know exactly how it would become a reality.

As the months went by, I went through so many transitions—the main one was moving back to Boston from Los Angeles. I stopped writing and forgot all about it, to be honest.

Three years later, on February 5, 2021, precisely, I was in my room, and landed on this lost file on my laptop. I opened it up, and as I read it, I could not even recognize what I had written. The more I read, I started to cry, and it hit me! I couldn't recognize what I had written because this was God through me! *Heaven on Earth* is what I had been asking God to reveal to me: the meaning of the words "Heaven on earth" that marked the day they were prophesied on my life.

Heaven on Earth was written to inspire, uplift, and support women's healing from heartbreak as I encourage them to lean on God and trust His plans.

I cried with so much gratitude and shock that God would use me in this way. I could not believe it took me four years to figure it out! From 2017 when it was prophesied on my life, to 2018 when I wrote it, to 2021 when I came across this lost file again and understood what it was.

I was not prepared to release this book in 2018 because I was not the person I am now—the healed, whole version of me. My relationship with God has grown so much, and I am now so much wiser. I am now the woman that God wanted me to become to publish His work.

In this book, you'll learn more about the relationship I was in and my walk of faith with God. I can officially say with confidence that I am healed and that God is so good! I am blessed, and I am the woman God has called me to be. He has blessed me and used me in so many ways that still blow me away, and he can do this for you, too. I cannot wait to see all the amazing lives He will impact through this book.

I am really excited to guide and help heal all who have experienced a similar season to mine. You are not alone. We are not alone, and never have been; He always is with us through it all.

Now, join me as we step into one of the darkest seasons in my life. As you read through, you will notice that there are dates I wrote in journal format as things came up for me during the breakup. You will find a mix of personal stories, with lessons referencing back to the Bible. Keep in mind, all throughout the session of this book that I am taking you back to moments from the past.

The Dry Place Is Not the Final Destination; It Is Just A Reference Point

January 10, 2018

It's 11:42 p.m., and I am finally taking the time to write this book after dwelling on it for so long. Today, I felt down and lost after waking up to a painful torn muscle in my back; I realized one year had passed since my grandmother died. My bank account has continued to shrink, and my income remains dismal. I'm living in California, lost about my career, my physical well-being, and my spiritual life.

I had always been aware of the presence of God and how important He is. I wouldn't have made it this far without Him. I grew up in the church; it was a non-negotiable for me. I'm grateful my parents instilled this in me. They made it clear how important it is to make church and God part of my everyday life. I steered away from the Lord's path for a season, thinking I could direct my own wheel, but I was wrong. However, I always kept God in mind, and it gave me a sense of hope through everything. I came back knowing that He was and will always be there waiting to heal, deliver, and strengthen me. My life would not be what it is now had I not known Him. He is my rock.

"Start children off on the way they should go, and even when they are old they will not turn from it"

(Proverbs 22:6).

Even if the child takes some detours, the child will often find his way back to the Lord as he has that awareness and knowledge about Him, which is what happened with me. In God, we find what the world cannot give us: peace, healing, and strength.

When We Deviate From God's Plans For Us, Things Happen

January 11, 2018

"There is a time for everything, and a season for every activity under the Heavens: a time to be born and a time to die, a time to plant and a time to uproot, a time to kill and a time to heal, a time to tear down and a time to build" (Ecclesiastes 3:1-3).

I dated someone for four years; he hid our relationship from his parents, so I hid it from my mother too. He did this not because of our age, as we were both twenty-one years old at the time, but because he came from a Muslim family and they wouldn't accept me—they wouldn't accept us. He was a very smart person with ambition, and I think that's what I loved most about him. He inspired me and I learned a lot about business and personal development from him. He was striving to become more and was not settling for less. He went from 0 to 100, literally from the bottom to (almost) the top. He started his own company and made the kind of money he wanted. I looked up to his dedication and hard work passionately.

Something was missing, though. Something always felt "off." As the months went by, my gut told me he wasn't being honest and that he was hiding things from me. I came across situations where he met with girls behind my back. He always had an excuse for it all—"recruitment purposes for the company" or something else. I chose to believe him even though it didn't feel right.

As the months went by, he traveled between San Francisco and Boston, and during those times, I felt this huge pain in my heart. I felt depressed, crying in my room out of nowhere every time he was away. I later found through my intuition (God) was speaking to me, warning me. He was cheating on me. He was great with his words, and he convinced me that my assumptions were wrong and the proof I had was not enough (messages, screenshots of hooker sites). I chose to believe him and give him another chance, only for him to do it again and again and again...I honestly lost count of how many times this happened during the four years that we were together. To this day, I do not know how I allowed so much disrespect. I was blinded by his potential. I believed that I would never find a man who I enjoyed doing life with as much as I did with him, and who was as hard-working and ambitious as me.

Meanwhile, I was praying for a sign from God. I asked God if this man was not for me, to remove him from my life because I could no longer deal with the pain and depression. I also prayed for a man who would love and respect me, worked out as much as I did, had muscles, and a beautiful smile with perfect teeth, but above all, someone who feared and honored God, and attended church every Sunday.

The Lord was speaking to me all along. The sadness, depression, and emptiness I felt with him were signs of God answering my prayers. His statement was clear: "He is not for you," but I didn't want to accept it.

This person wasn't doing any regular sort of cheating (if there is even such a thing). He cheated on me with prostitutes. He had a sexual problem. From the moment the relationship started and he kept us a secret from his family, I knew it wouldn't go anywhere. Deep down I knew all along he was not the man God had for me, but I allowed the devil to convince me otherwise.

I can't explain the pain that I've felt from everything that I experienced with him. I was sleeping with the devil. I had sleepless nights; I woke up in the middle of the night choking, feeling like I couldn't breathe—I was having panic attacks from replaying every situation in my head. The things he had put me through, the lies he had told me, and while we were still together, the possible things he could still be doing.

I pray that no woman allows herself to get to that point. I pray that you follow the Holy Spirit; it is trying to protect you, and never fails you. Therefore, learn how to listen to it, please, and do not go against God's will. Remove all distractions and noise, create a sacred place in your home to come and connect with God on a daily basis through prayer, and surrender it all to Him. He will guide you. Pray about every decision and every man who comes into your life. Ask God if this is the man He has for you, and then be still and listen. Pay attention to the feeling you get. This is really important because how it makes you feel will determine if it is the right relationship or not. Do you feel joy and peace? Or do you feel sad, depressed, or not valued?

I didn't do any of that before getting in this relationship and I ended up dancing with the devil, but thank God I have been delivered. He had cheated on me for the last time, and I truly had enough. At that point, I had been praying for deliverance and for another incident to happen so that it could give me the strength to leave him for good because the times he had cheated on me in the past were not enough for me to walk away.

Sometimes It Takes an Overwhelming Breakdown to Have an Undeniable Breakthrough

January 12, 2018

Exactly a year ago today was a very difficult time for me. It was my mother's birthday, but my grandmother had just passed away two days prior, so there was no spirit of celebration. I was also dealing with the usual cheating problems with my now-ex, so he was not around for the times I needed him the most.

Losing my grandmother was the most painful thing that had ever happened to me. She was like my second mother; she raised me along with my mother. I saw her grow old as she saw me grow up. As the days went by and I was slowly starting to recover from everything, one of my girls invited me to her church for a women's-only service. At the end of that service, Pastor Ivette Monge called each girl individually on stage to sit on a chair as she crowned them and prophesied to them.

I was the last one to go up. The very first thing she said as I sat on that chair was, "I don't know what you've lost, but it has caused you a lot of pain to your stomach." As she said that, I felt my heart sink to my stomach and I began to cry with so much pain. I felt like I couldn't breathe. Then she said, "BUT God will fill your heart with joy and he will fulfill all of the desires of your heart. A new season is to come; you have something very special. You will bring Heaven on earth."

As I left, I kept asking myself...Heaven on earth? Heaven on earth? What does this mean? I called my mom and told her about it, and how it felt good to hear that. It gave me hope and I could not wait to find out what it meant. Meanwhile, I continued to play with fire...I was still entertaining my ex-boyfriend's antics.

I believe that my blessing has been delayed because I was still putting up with him. It's been about a year since that prophecy, and I still can't seem to find out what "Heaven on earth" means. I am still praying on it.

I moved to California in hopes of leaving the past in the past, leaving the pain, and starting fresh. After my grandmother's death, things were different at home. I thought moving would also be good in terms of the unhealthy relationship with my ex. I thought I would be strong enough to leave him, but the cards didn't play quite as I planned...he ended up leaving Boston and moving in with me in California, which dragged things out that much longer. I still hadn't learned my lesson.

For the four years we were together, he would mess up to make up. He would go for about two months being good (at least I thought), and then I would catch him again. He did it every other month. I was finally able to walk away because at that point, God had told me so many times that he is not the man for me, yet I continued to open the door he had already shut for me. It took a while but I was finally in agreement that I had to let go for my own well-being and to be in alignment with what God wants for me, not my own desires.

It has also been very challenging being away from my family and finding myself career-wise, too. I'm crying to God for strength and healing as I'm in so much pain, and I feel so lost. I question why I've had to go through so much but I know there is a higher purpose for this all.

I did just discover a Church called The Potter's House at OneLA. After going to many churches in hopes of finding one that made me feel at home, I felt this was it the moment I stepped foot inside. Worship is really important for me; I need my time to worship and to be in God's beautiful presence before I can feed off His Word, and this Church gave me that. I was so used to my good ol' Jubilee back in Boston. Their worship team is everything! It is so hard to compare to them. But The Potter's House at OneLA was quite there!

I want you to know that you are not alone; the devil wants you to believe that you are, but that is not the truth. There are women all over the world facing similar things like us.

You need to be strong and recognize what is worth fighting for and what is best to simply let go of. If it is stealing your peace, your joy, your sanity, you need to walk away! Before we broke up, I was at the point where I could not sleep in peace. I always wanted to go through his phone, and even when he wasn't home, I wanted to FaceTime him to make sure he wasn't up to anything that he "shouldn't" be up to. I was miserable, all of that because I wanted to salvage our relationship so badly, and perhaps not be alone.

Those feelings, as reflected in my journal entries, lasted far beyond the end of our relationship, but it didn't have to be that way. I could have stopped opening doors God had closed, but in pain, there is often a lesson or something good that can come of it. We can't always see it at the time, but in retrospect, it becomes clear. That, for me, resulted in this book to help other women experiencing heartbreak.

Pain Is Inevitable; It's How You Choose to Heal That Matters

January 13, 2018

I have experienced so much pain in the last few years between my grandmother's passing and this relationship. I no longer knew what peace was. I had been so mentally disturbed by the things he did to me; I was going crazy every time I took him back. I felt so suffocated, and that is when I knew I had to take action before it became too late.

It had already been four years. How much longer could I do this? Shortly before we broke up, God was telling me it was now or never. I had already gone against His will this whole time and I knew that because I had lost the most precious thing in my life—peace. Every day that went by, every hour, every minute, every second that I stayed in the relationship, I continued to replay the memories of the betrayal experienced during those four years.

I was looking for healing in the same place that I had been broken, and that was very difficult to find as that place continued to be dark and took away from me, leaving a feeling of emptiness and sadness, of trauma.

God did not create me to live in depression and fear, nor in a relationship where I am not respected. God created me to know my worth. None of what I experienced is meaningless. I believe it was necessary to allow me to become the strong, powerful being that God has called me to be.

Depression is necessary to appreciate joy. The tears are necessary to appreciate healing. The lack of love is necessary to appreciate genuine, pure love in its abundance. Disloyalty is necessary to appreciate loyalty. The storm is necessary to appreciate the sunshine.

Nothing in this world would be appreciated if we didn't experience unpleasant things. We must experience these things so that we are clear on the things we want more of in our lives. Otherwise, there would be no meaning to anything. We need to experience the ugly so we know that we never want to be there again. This is how we value the better—knowing what it's like on the other side.

If You Don't Change the Situation, Your Situation Will Change You

January 14, 2018

Every time I left him before I finally walked away, I got a feeling of relief; it was like a burden had been removed from my back and I could finally breathe again.

Of course, I initially felt so much pain, sadness, and anger, especially now that it's officially over for good. But I'm handing it over to the Lord. I'm going to continue to work on myself—I realize I have a lot of healing to do. I've started working ten times harder on my physical, spiritual, and financial well-being. I started taking my workouts to the next level, going to church twice a week, and I started writing this book, aside from my other business, as that is what I feel the Lord wants me to do. I've always had the desire to uplift women spiritually, physically, and mentally.

Every time I previously took my ex back, I would steer away from God. I guess the reason was that I felt ashamed. I felt like I kept letting God down because I would ask Him to deliver and rescue me from the relationship but I wouldn't allow Him to; I refused to let go.

The four years with him were really a challenge for me, but I realize now that that is because I had been going against God's will. I didn't love myself, but I craved to be loved...so badly. I was determined to help him become the man I thought he could be—a loyal, loving, honest boyfriend, fiancé, and perhaps husband.

Many of us will block our blessings by being in a place where God has already declared isn't the place for us. We believe that by trying to control a man, he will change; we believe that we can stop him from doing the things he wants to do by monitoring his every move. If he intends to do something, he will find a way no matter what. This relationship got to the point where he was sharing his location on his phone with me, I had his passwords to everything... and he still cheated. He still found a way. All he had to do was stop sharing his location (tell me his phone died, froze on him, etc.) and go about his business.

If you cannot trust the person you are with, you should re-evaluate why you are in a relationship. Without trust, there is nothing. It'll drive you to lose your peace and that is when things tend to get ugly. It'll bring out another side of you fueled by anger, fear, and the need for control. I used to have panic attacks at night because I was always trying to stop him from cheating on me. That is not the way to live. Peace is the most beautiful thing you can experience in life. Peace is so valuable, and without peace, we lose ourselves.

The right man will not give you any reasons to try to monitor or control his every move because you will know that you can trust him no matter what, and that he will never do anything to jeopardize the relationship. I've always said I want a partner who if one day someone were to approach me and tell me that he cheated on me, I can confidently stand by him knowing that they've got the wrong guy, and I would be right. Every woman knows her man; your gut always let you know. My gut always told me that he wasn't the man for me and that he was always up to something when he wasn't with me. He was a completely different human being when not in my presence. My gut was right all along; that gut feeling was really a prompting from the Holy Spirit.

I was centered on him; my whole world revolved around him to the point where I forgot about myself. The wrong relationship will drain you. Don't let the fear of leaving cause you to ignore the pain in staying. My pastor, Sarah Jakes Roberts, once said, "If you don't change the situation, your situation will change you."

Never confuse what you are offered with what you are worth. Pray for wisdom, that the Lord may reveal to you who is worth fighting for and who isn't, who is sent by Him and who isn't, who has good intentions with you, and who doesn't. "Is this the man you have sent for me, Lord? Show me otherwise."

Being a Christian

January 15, 2018

What God has revealed to me during this season is that there is so much more to being a Christian than just going to church. Some people go to church for mere entertainment and motivation, but going to church is about feeding our minds and souls. It's about going to church with the intent to practice and apply what is being taught after leaving the building.

Being a Christian isn't just about going to church on Sundays. Yes, we go to church every Sunday, but there is so much more that we get to practice outside of the church to keep our souls in alignment with God throughout the week. We need to pray, fast, worship, and meditate on His Word. God isn't something we use when we are down and need some "motivation." We seek God for deliverance and guidance. We must sacrifice certain things in our lives in order to receive His guidance and help. How can we expect God to be with us if we can go days without talking to Him, without being in His presence? I know it's easier to go to God in times when we most need Him especially when we are torn, broken, and need hope. But we must go to Him in times of rain and sunshine.

A lot of people say it is easier to praise the Lord when things are good, but people tend to forget about God when times are good because they think they don't need Him at that point. Consider this: How messed up would it be if we heard from a friend only in their times of need and she never reached out when times were good? Just because we don't see Him and we can't actually hear His voice does not mean we should treat Him lesser than we treat humans. We need to treat God, our Savior, with a lot more love and respect. He is the Most High. He is always there when we need Him. A human being wouldn't accept a friendship that worked only in times of need, but God is all love and forgiveness. Seek Him in good and in bad.

"Rejoice in the Lord always. I will say it again: Rejoice!" (Philippians 4:4).

"I'm Not Perfect"

January 16, 2018

A lot of us like to say, "Well, I'm not perfect" when we sin. That is a mere excuse so that we can feel better going about our days sinning without even attempting to fight the urge of temptation. The devil is a liar, and that is what the devil wants you to believe. Yes, of course, we are not perfect, but when we lean on God, He gives us strength and we can do our best to practice His will with the intention of perfection. We cannot go about our days saying, "Oh, no problem. I will take one hit, I will take one sip, I will have sex with my boyfriend—everyone else does it, and I'm not perfect."

I'm not saying I've never been there before; yes, I have, but the Holy Spirit spoke to me and told me that doing these things is not the right way of living through God. We are either all in or we are all out! God does *not* like half efforts. Just like we demand *all* from our partners, He demands *all* from us. Choose your path, and if you can't figure it out, pray about it!

Quick Prayer: Lord, be my sight, be my language, overtake my thoughts, overtake my actions, and overtake my feelings. Forgive me of all of my sins.

Fight Your Battles on Your Knees

January 17, 2018

Alot of people just know me as Irene, the awesome, happy girl who is always so cheerful, so positive, and so hard working. But what they don't see is how much fighting I do on my knees; they don't know the struggles and the pain I've endured. As the Bible reads, "But when you pray, go into your room, close the door and pray to your Father, who is unseen. Then your Father, who sees what is done in secret, will reward you"

(Matthew 6:6).

Fight your battles on your knees, and do it in private. All people can see is that you are being blessed, and you are highly favored, but it is all because of your sacrifices for Him. He loves it when we spend intimate time with Him and lean on Him through our circumstances.

"Be joyful in hope, patient in affliction, faithful in prayer" (Romans 12:12).

You will bless generations through your prayers now. Your prayers today will trickle down to your whole family—your children, your grandchildren, your great-grandchildren. Never stop praying, no matter what season you are in. Continue praying and sacrificing for the Lord.

Take Your Burdens to the Lord

Today, I was so overwhelmed, I felt like I was going to burst, and I couldn't wait to run home to go into my prayer room and let it all out. The devil tried to tempt me again with my past. I saw something I shouldn't have seen that brought back a memory of my ex, whom I've been trying to stay away from. This hurt me, and aside from that, I am struggling financially. I feel like I'm not surrounded by the right like-minded spiritual people, and I am away from the people I love the most—my mom, my brother, and my dog. I carry so much pain, stress, and uncertainty.

The Bible reads, "Cast your cares on the Lord and he will sustain you; he will never let the righteous be shaken" (Psalm 55:22).

The moment I felt that way, I remembered this verse, and I could not wait to let it all out and just ask the Lord to take all of my burdens so that I could feel peace and calmness. I know that He has my back and He will take care of things. He already has a plan and that plan is to provide for me. He will never leave me or forsake me: "Be strong and courageous. Do not be afraid or terrified because of them, for the Lord your God goes with you; he will never leave you nor forsake you"

(Deuteronomy 31:6).

Wounded People Hurt; Healed People Spread Love

January 18, 2018

I eventually came to the realization that my ex truly had a problem. As I began to understand more, I cried so much because I felt so sad that I could not help him overcome that problem. But I prayed and I knew that God would be the only one who could help him—not me or anyone else.

"Do to others as you would have them do to you"

(Luke 6:31).

Be the person you want to attract. Be the person you want to date. Be the person you want in your life as a friend, as a sister, as a daughter, as a family member, colleague, wife, or as the mother figure you wish you had.

Before you say "no" to someone's request for support, think about what you wish would happen if you were in his or her situation. Who you are, what you do, and what you say are reflections of you and what is going on in your heart. People who love themselves are joyful in the name of Jesus Christ and do not hurt other people or hate on others. They

spread nothing but love and hope. Those who are always in a miserable state of mind are wounded and hurt, which is why they cannot give the world anything but hate and hurt. The Bible says, "But to you who are listening I say: Love your enemies, do good to those who hate you, bless those who curse you, pray for those who mistreat you"

(Luke 6:27-28).

Therefore, whoever is tormenting you, whether it's at work, in relationships, friendships, family members...make sure you pray for them and ask God to heal them from whatever it is that they are dealing with because it has nothing to do with you—it is a battle they are fighting within themselves.

Pray for those who hurt you. Pray they find healing. It may be hard to understand, but everyone is fighting his or her own individual battles and traumas. I repeat, pray for them; it has nothing to do with you.

Continue Doing Good No Matter What

"Let us not become weary in doing good, for at the proper time we will reap a harvest if we do not give up" (Galatians 6:9).

I always had a hard time understanding why my mother was so kind, loving, and forgiving to people, oftentimes to the people I was upset with, either because there was a record of bad history between them and us (e.g., family members) or a friend of hers who just didn't reciprocate her kindness. Many times, she would have people over and give them food to take home, or she would constantly give a friend or coworker a ride to work and back, or she would lend money without expecting it back.

I would question her actions and asked her why she would constantly go out of her way to do such things for others. She always said, "Irene, don't worry. What I do here will be compensated in Heaven. Good deeds always come back. I enjoy being good to others." This always left me astounded, yet I have witnessed many miracles in my mother's life because of this, me being one of them.

I say me being one of them because realistically, I shouldn't have turned out to be who I am. Growing up without a father, my mother always worked two jobs to provide, I had no one disciplining me and guiding me to adulthood. I barely graduated from high school; I took myself to college (no one told me I had to go to college, never mind how to find financial help for it). I taught myself everything I know now. How did I not just throw my life away? God's favor.

My mom did always make sure I knew that God existed, and she made sure I built a relationship with Him. She taught me that God is everything, and I shall always seek Him. Regardless of what she wasn't able to teach me at an early age, this is the greatest thing she could have ever gifted me with. It is the most vital thing I needed in my life to survive...all I needed to survive.

I am a harvest of what my mother has sown through her acts of serving and giving. Her obedience and faithfulness to God have allowed her to be abundant and overflowing in blessings. Because of her I am so highly favored by God.

Take this as a lesson in perseverance and humility. Continue doing good, even in those times, you may not feel like it.

The Greatest Things Come Into Your Life Through Sacrifice & Inconvenience

January 19, 2018

"But the fruit of the Spirit is love, joy, peace, forbearance, kindness, goodness, faithfulness, gentleness, and self-control. Against such things, there is no law. Those who belong to Christ Jesus have crucified the flesh with its passions and desires"

(Galatians 5:22-24).

When I read this Scripture, I knew that God wanted me to give up one thing. This is the moment I decided I needed to take sexual purity seriously. I knew I had to make a promise not to have sex until marriage. I knew that there was such a big blessing behind all of this. "Therefore, I urge you, brothers and sisters, in view of God's mercy, to offer your bodies as a living sacrifice, holy and pleasing to God—this is your true and proper worship" (Romans 12:1). Wow, this spoke to my soul!

I want to please God with all of my soul, all of my heart, with everything I have. I crave to please Him and to be righteous. I've lived in the wrong, going against His will for too long. I know what it's like to live without His protection, and that's a place I never want to be in again, and I never will be again in the name of Jesus Christ, for I am His child and I belong in His path. I will never let go of His hand till He blesses my soul, and even then, I will still hold on tight.

The greatest things are going to come into your life through sacrifice and inconvenience. There cannot be a relationship without inconvenience. The problem with culture today? Instant gratification. We want everything fast and easy. If you won't do it through inconvenience, you really don't want it because nothing great will ever happen through convenience.

A lot of people want to follow Jesus on their terms; they no longer know how to sacrifice because it is an inconvenience to them.

You have to choose your destination. You're either going to obey God and truly practice His Word, or you will continue to live freely in the world by your own desires. Perhaps you are doing good deeds but still living in sin. This does not please God as you continue to live by the flesh. There is so much more to being a Christian—everything from sacrifices to fasting, from tithing to obeying His Word, from reading His Word to teaching others about Him. The more you practice these things, the closer you get to Him, and the further you get from feeding into the desires of the flesh.

"Not everyone who says to me, 'Lord, Lord,' will enter the kingdom of Heaven, but only the one who does the will of my Father who is in Heaven"

(Matthew 7:21).

I am not one hundred percent where I should be yet. God is still working on me, but I am definitely making the effort to do the right thing. Starting by choosing abstinence, generating a holy mouth, to simply being the best person I can be. I refrain from criticizing or judging people. I refrain from talking about people. There is power in everything that comes out of our mouths so use your words wisely.

"The tongue has the power of life and death, and those who love it will eat its fruit"

(Proverbs 18:21).

Every Transformation Always Gets Worse Before It Gets Better

January 20, 2018

You getting up, swinging, and missing—that is progress.
The effort of making the attempt is what matters.
If you keep pushing and seeking God, it will happen!

I ask God every day to deliver me from every position that is hindering me. I want Him to fulfill His purpose in my life and I pray that He removes all jealousy, confusion, insecurities, hate, and anger, if any. My heart is His home and therefore, none of that belongs here, just healing, peace, joy, certainty, confidence, and love.

"Looking at his disciples, he said: 'Blessed are you who are poor, for yours is the kingdom of God. Blessed are you who hunger now, for you will be satisfied. Blessed are you who weep now, for you will laugh" (Luke 6:20-21).

He will give us everything we need. He will provide. He will give us the fulfillment we have been seeking in the world, in that man, that friend, that person—whomever or whatever it may have been—we were looking for it in the wrong place. God is the only one who can give us fulfillment. The drugs won't, the sex won't, the alcohol won't, the party won't, nothing and nobody **but God.**

Do not allow the past to define who you are or where you are going. The devil wants you to dwell on the past; he will continue to bring up the past to keep you from healing and receiving better. Do not allow him to win. I allowed him to win many times, but not this last time. This last time was different. I allowed the Lord to intercede. I allowed Him to take over my life, my burdens, my struggles, and my pain. I stopped wanting to manipulate things my way. Instead, I allowed it to be God's will. I allowed the breakup to happen. I allowed it to stay there as I prayed for God to give me the strength to move forward and not look back.

I cried out to the Lord for His strength every single day. It was so painful, but I had to choose to believe that the pain I felt was temporary. I had to remember that God has a purpose and a greater plan for my life.

Prayer

January 21, 2018

I pray that You bring me out of the darkness, and I pray that You bring light into my life. I'm tired of living in pain, living in the dark. I am Your child, and healing, joy, peace, and prosperity belong to me. Deliver me from this, Jesus.

The devil keeps trying to attack me by bringing the past back up in my life, and it is very painful. I cried out to God to remove every feeling and every memory that I have of my ex, and I am still trying to let go of all the hate that I have for him because it does not support my relationship with God—it is hindering it.

I always tell God that I forgive my ex. He didn't ask for forgiveness and I don't want to forgive him, but I get to do it because that is what God wants me to do. He is a forgiving God and we get to forgive because He forgives us always.

It's really hard for me to understand all of this pain and depression. I feel like I have nobody to run to but God, and sometimes I wish I could simply get a hug and be told that everything is going to be okay. Yet I know things are going to be okay because God is with me, and He has promised to never leave me or forsake me. I just want all of this pain and hate to be removed from my heart. My heart belongs to God.

I pray that whatever struggles you are going through, may the Lord bring light, show you the way, and heal you. I pray that whatever you are fighting, you bring it to your prayer room. The best battles are fought on your knees, bringing your burdens and struggles to the cross as I did in this journal entry.

I pray that none of you allow yourselves to get to where I was. Don't ever tolerate anything that has to do with lies, cheating, or any sort of abuse—anything that disrespects you because those things do not support God's vision for your life.

If It Feels Wrong, It's Because It Is... Trust Your Gut (Holy Spirit)!

January 22, 2018

Pay attention to the feeling you get in certain situations and with certain people. The emptiness you feel, the discomfort you feel, is the Holy Spirit trying to reach out to you. It's the Holy Spirit screaming, "Run! He is not for you! He will hurt you!" You must learn how to listen to the Holy Spirit; this is the greatest gift God has left with us to guide us, protect us, and warn us when something isn't right. You don't know how many times the Holy Spirit has saved me from big troubles! This relationship was the only exception, but that's because I chose to go against that feeling.

The Holy Spirit is our best friend. The Holy Spirit protects us. Thankfully, Jesus is always waiting with open arms, waiting to catch us and pick us back up. The devil cannot hold us down.

I pray that you never go into a relationship without praying to God about it first. If it doesn't feel right, it's because it isn't. Listen to the Holy Spirit. It never fails you.

We All Have a Choice

January 23, 2018

Just like there is light and dark, there is good and bad, love and hate, Heaven and hell. We must learn how to distinguish these. We must learn how to make wise choices. Life would be too easy if we didn't have to put in work for the good and worthy things.

Easy or hard? Which path would you pick if you knew the most difficult path would bring you so much more reward at the end?

The Bible reads, "Enter through the narrow gate, for wide is the gate and broad is the road that leads to destruction, and many enter through it. But small is the gate and narrow the road that leads to *life* and *only a few* find it" (Matthew 7:13-14, emphasis added).

For example, everyone wants the "perfect relationship," but only a few are willing to do the work. Everyone wants God's blessings, but not everyone is willing to make sacrifices and live for Him.

In order to have the healthy relationship we desire, we must work on healing all of our wounds and traumas, and that may get uncomfortable. In order to have God's favor, we must give up certain things that tie us to the world, which may not be so easy, but do not choose the easy, comfortable route. The comfortable route will lead you into the wide gate, and this road usually brings destruction and pulls you away from God. Make decisions that lead you to the narrow road; this road is usually a more challenging lifestyle as we get to make some sacrifices. However, it is the most rewarding path, and God guides us every step of the way if we allow Him to.

Take a leap of faith and do not stay in a relationship because of comfort.

The Meaning of Life

January 24, 2018

To me, the meaning of life is going through experiences that we learn from. Whether they are beautiful moments or the most painful, I believe that it is all for our development and growth. There is purpose in our pain. We may not understand the "why" behind everything that happens at the moment, but once time goes by and you look back, you have a better understanding of why those doors were shut, why you were hurt the way you were, why that relationship didn't work out, why you lost the job, why you didn't get the part—the dots start to connect. It's about learning and growing.

Ask God for wisdom and you'll start to understand that all of what life puts us through will make us a better person, a better girlfriend, a better friend, a better daughter, a better sister, a better employee, etc. Try not to question what happens but to understand the "why" behind it, accepting that it's happening *for* you, not to you.

Life is very beautiful when you learn to walk with God and understand that He has a purpose for your life. His intention is not to leave you where you are; He intends to lift you up and use your pain for something greater. This that you are going through is preparing you for what He has in store for you. God is simply waiting for you to call on His name and invite Him in. His ways are higher than ours. Trust that He's got you!

"Things which do not grow and learn are dead."

–Louis Erdrich

Pain Is Necessary

January 25, 2018

Sometimes, God closes doors because it's time to move forward. He knows you won't move unless your circumstances force you to. God does not plan to harm you; however, He will allow certain things to happen due to disobedience and ongoing sin. God chooses to allow us to learn the consequences.

"Know then in your heart that as a man disciplines his son, so the Lord your God disciplines you"

(Deuteronomy 8:5).

God knows our strength. Therefore, the storm will be a catalyst for growth. The pain of losses will give us an appreciation for all of our achievements and experiences. The act of falling will allow us to practice getting up, and this is vital to life because the devil wants to keep us on the ground. He wants us to lose the battle. He wants us to think that pain is all there is, and that is *the* storm.

I had to go through the unhealthiest relationship to know my worth, to love myself enough, to know what I should never accept in my life, and what you shouldn't accept in your life, either. I had to go through this relationship to know what it's like for other women in similar unhealthy relationships and to be able to help them through it. We are not alone. *You are not alone*. You are the child of God, and He wants—and has—the best plans for you. You just have to stay still! Do not interrupt the plans He has for you. Trust His plans! Trust the process.

God Listens and Answers Prayers

January 26, 2018

I was at church today and Sarah Jakes gave such an amazing message that really touched my soul. It clarified to me that I am on the right path and that this book is meant to be written, for His glory, not for me, but for Him, in the name of Jesus Christ. God is going to use me to speak to many of you beautiful women who are weary, fighting a battle that isn't even yours, with a man who isn't for you.

At the end of the service, Sarah called for an altar prayer. I ran down because I felt like that message was for me! As we prayed, I started to cry. I was so in tune with the presence of the Holy Spirit. As the prayer was over and I was about to walk back to my seat, this beautiful girl named Ericka approached me and said, "I just wanted to let you know that God wants me to tell you that everything is going to be okay, and that you are stronger than you think."

I was not expecting this, but it was exactly at the right time, and I hugged her. I really needed to hear that at that moment because I was feeling so weak and lost with everything in my life. I needed guidance, and there He was. God spoke to me through this beautiful young girl. She also gifted me a book, which oddly I had been looking into getting but circumstances didn't allow me to, and then I knew why. He wanted to use her as a blessing for my life. God is so amazing; He will always place people in your life for your growth and healing.

God will start sending people your way who will lift you up. When you least expect it, He will show up—whether it's through a word, a person, a dream, whatever it is, in whatever form. He will show up for you.

Focus on the Good and the Good Gets Better

January 27, 2018

"Make a tree good and its fruits will be good, or make a tree bad and its fruit will be bad, for a tree is recognized by its fruit"

(Matthew 12:33).

Where focus goes, energy flows, or perhaps I attracted these people, or encouraged them to not be ashamed to love God. The moment I started posting about my love and faith for God, most of my followers started messaging me telling me that they loved how open I was about my relationship with God, without shame, and how they also loved and trusted in the Lord. Whatever it was, I was extremely happy that it was happening. I wanted to be used by God and share His amazing presence with everyone because He is great and worthy to be praised. And life is so much better with Him!

The moment I started focusing on my relationship with God and with myself, I started encountering people who also loved the Lord. I would encourage you to never be afraid to share what God has done for you. Your testimony is important, and you never know whose life may be impacted by it.

Trust Him

January 28, 2018

"For I know the plans I have for you,' declares the LORD, 'plans to prosper you and not to harm you, plans to give you hope and a future"

(Jeremiah 29:11).

Trust in Him. Understand that what He has is greater than you can imagine. His plans are greater than yours. Better than the plans we have for ourselves. Don't question the doors that have been shut; He has shut them, and that means everything. God doesn't close a door without opening a new one—for every ending, there is a new beginning. Pray for new doors to open in your favor, doors that no man can shut because God opened them, and that means they will be of great blessings and purpose for your life.

God listens, watches, and digests. He analyzes your prayers with your actions. In some instances, people pray for things but they don't truly want them. They will pray for a good man but remain sleeping with the devil. They will pray for that idea, but then they are scared to take action, even when it is God telling them to do it. They ask for love but give hate. They ask for honesty but tell lies. "In the same way, faith by itself, if it is not accompanied by action, is DEAD" (James 2:17, emphasis added). Match your prayers with action!

God Will Change Your Plans Sometimes

January 29, 2018

I made plans to move to California thinking that this is where He wanted me to be, where I would find my purpose, and where it would be fulfilled. I did find my purpose, but I don't believe this is where it is going to be fulfilled.

I met with the CEO of a gym I visited today, and as this person spoke to me and tried to sell me on being a health coach in his company, it all clicked in my head. I've been meditating on the idea of opening up a gym, but something keeps telling me that it should not be in California, that I should open it up in Boston.

I already know so many people in Boston who have come to me for health tips because they've witnessed my fitness journey, and I also know my whole hometown would support me. During that meeting, I felt like God was confirming that. He wants me to go to Boston and open up this fitness center and change people's lives.

My plans were to be in California and do other things with my life, but He has different plans for me, and I will follow them because I want His will done in my life. No matter how much I love California, I have to leave; hopefully, it will be temporary, until I have things up and running in Boston. All I know is that this is His will for my life, His plan in which a big blessing lies, and I shall receive it in His name.

My dreams scare me; my dreams seem so impossible to me, but I trust that they are actually very possible with God.

Many people will block their blessings by simply not allowing God to take over and guide them through what He has planned for them. We can be so stubborn in our ways in wanting to do what we want, no matter what He says, and that is when we fail, or rather, miss out on His blessings for our lives—His beautiful perfect plan. Trust Him; He will take you there...

"Jesus looked at them and said, 'With man this is impossible, but with God all things are possible"

(Matthew 19:26).

Fear only exists in our heads, and the best things are usually on the other side of fear. Do not allow fear to stop you from going after your dreams. Ask God to deliver you from any fear getting in the way of His plans. Fear is something that the devil tries to attack you with. Rebuke it from your life; God's children shall not fear.

"Have I not commanded you? Be strong and courageous. Do not be afraid; do not be discouraged, for the Lord your God will be with you wherever you go"

(Joshua 1:9).

God is so amazing, and He continues to impress me every day. He is always looking out for us, whether you see it at the moment or not.

If it hurts, trust that it is temporary.
If the door was shut, trust that it was Him.
If you feel lost, trust that He will find you and guide you.
If you are confused, trust that He will give you certainty.
If you are blind, trust that He will give you a vision.
If you are wounded, trust that He will heal you.
If you feel empty, trust that He will fill you up!

Epilogue: Faith

February 25, 2021

Three years later...I listened to God and moved back to Boston. It's midnight. I am lying in bed, my mind was blown, in tears of amazement and joy by God's *perfect will and plans.*

I started writing this book back in January 2018, but I stopped writing that same year as I moved back to Boston, forgetting all about it. The night of February 5, 2021, something triggered the memory of this book, so I opened the file and as I read it, I could not believe all that I had written. That's when I knew it had been God using me to write with Him. At that moment, clarity came to me: *This* is Heaven on earth. I finally figured out the meaning of Heaven on earth!

God asked me to uplift and empower women through this book as I teach them about Him, His will, and His amazing miracles and love. God has shown up for me in so many ways and has fulfilled all of His promises in my life. Above all, I trusted Him through it all, and I never doubted His plans.

I trusted the Holy Spirit, obeyed God's will, and moved to Boston after praying for so long about my purpose and calling. I did indeed *find* my purpose in California, but the calling to *fulfill* that purpose was in Boston.

My calling in life is to empower, transform, and support women's healing; it started through fitness and has expanded to a different mindset and spiritual aspects. God gifted me a gym. Many people on the way told me I could never own a gym and that it was nearly impossible or just too hard. I now own a successful fitness facility. I have hosted women's retreats, I impact and empower women as I envisioned, and I am now a published author. God's beautiful plan has unfolded.

I never imagined any of this was possible, but it happened, and it happened because I chose to trust God, be obedient, and follow His will. I knew in my heart that He wanted me to move back home, and I am so glad I did. God has blessed me beyond imagination here.

God is so good. Every rejection, every failure, and the painful breakup that started it all led me in the right direction. I am exactly where I was meant to be; the pain was necessary.

Sacrifice for Him, do as He asks, and trust that once you let go of what isn't for you, He will bless you with greater than you can imagine. I went from being broke, having no purpose in life, not loving myself, being with someone who represented all of that, and being depressed, to now walking and living in my purpose. I have found peace like no other. I feel fulfilled and joyful, but most importantly, I found the peace that I so deeply desired for so long, and that is *priceless.*

My desires and dreams scared me then, and they continue to scare me, but my faith has grown so much since 2018 as I survived the heartbreak, survived being lost in life, by allowing Him to guide me through it all. I am a living testimony that when you let Him guide you and you do as He asks, He will bless you! He will heal you! He will provide for you! He will fulfill His ultimate purpose in you. I feel at peace and confident that I shall never worry about the future, knowing I've got the best mentor in my life.

I hope this book brings a little bit of Heaven to you—hope and light to your situation. Seek Him and He shall deliver you and provide for you.

"The lions may grow weak and hungry, but those who seek the LORD lack no good thing"

(Psalm 34:10).

One last thing I'd like to emphasize is to *truly* trust the process.

"No discipline seems pleasant at the time, but painful. Later on, however, it produces a harvest of righteousness and peace for those who have been trained by it"

(Hebrews 12:11).

It is all happening for us. As painful as it may get at times, continue seeking the Lord, and at the end, you will harvest the blessings and peace from all the pain, the healing from all the wounds.

It took me a total of five years of trials and tribulations, a lot of pain and losses, and now finally this past year has been the most fruitful and rewarding year of my life. I have become the woman God has been preparing me to become. I would not be this version of me had I not gone through the process of discipline with God.

This isn't the last of my trials. For every new level, there is a new devil. There will be many trials throughout our lives, but keep in mind that the only way out is through. Keep your faith and trust in God. This too shall pass, and you shall reap the harvest of peace once you arrive at your destination.

Trust that there is light at the end of the tunnel.

Overcoming The Breakup

For me, it took a strong desire and willpower to want to be in control of my life again and live for God. Aside from praying and crying out to God for healing, I watched YouTube videos all day on tips for how to overcome a breakup and heal, I read books, and I hired a breakup life coach. I worked with her for the first three months; she helped me get out of the breakup funk and shift the energy into my business and myself. I kept myself super busy with work, and to be honest, my business started thriving more than ever.

But most importantly, I allowed myself to feel every emotion. I allowed myself to be sad and feel the pain, but I did not stay there. I knew I had to move on, and I had to love myself enough to walk away, so I did the work. I was willing to do whatever it took to detach myself from the relationship and give myself the attention I needed, which was *self-love*.

I started to feel better about five or six months later; I started healing. Know that it will take time, and that amount of time will be different for everyone. This shift happened the moment I chose to let go of the anger I was holding on to. The anger turned into compassion and from there, I felt a strong sense of freedom. The anger and hatred toward him were holding me back from healing, and weighing me down. Now, I understand why people say forgiving isn't about the other person—it's about you. Holding on to the anger was only hurting me. At the twelve-month mark, I truly felt completely healed and no longer felt pain over what I had lived through.

The freedom and joy I felt were so astonishing! You can experience this, too. It's such a huge accomplishment when you get here because being in the process feels like you'll never see the light again. Or like you're slowly sinking in the ocean—yet the moment you let go of what was dragging you down, you are released. You reach the top and eagerly gasp for some air, you can now breathe again. Diamonds are created under pressure; the process may get ugly but the outcome is so worth it.

The year I spent healing has been the most beautiful part of the journey. I feel so empowered, so free, so full; I feel unstoppable and so much stronger. I feel confident about the future and nothing can break me.

So, do the work. Love yourself enough to give you what you deserve. You are the only person who gets to dictate the story of your life. You are worthy.

Was It Him or You?

You were not the problem. However, it is important to look at who in your family demonstrated the behavior you modeled in this relationship. Who in your life has accepted betrayal, cheating, and lies? Who in your life made it normal to accept this kind of behavior in a partner?

People seek what is familiar. If in our past, we witnessed our parents going through this and they accepted similar behavior, then *we* tend to accept it. If in our past we felt inadequate or not enough, we are drawn to scenarios in which we feel the same way as adults, and our actions and ways of supporting those all-too-familiar feelings of being inadequate and undeserving.

The better we understand ourselves and our behavior, the better we'll be able to let go of this pattern.

Know your worth. You can't be afraid to lose them more than you are afraid to lose yourself.

If you would like to do some deeper work to gain clarity on your wounds and the life you desire and deserve, download our FREE workbook:

www.heavenonearthwb.com/free

Acknowledgments

Acknowledgemnt of My Childhood Wound

The truth is that all I've ever wanted was to just feel important to a man, to feel loved and wanted by a man.

I never had my father in my life. I never met him. He died before I could even get a chance...before I could get any answers as to why he was never in my life, why he never looked for me.

This was my childhood wound and what played a part in me choosing to settle for something that wasn't love, choosing to stay in a relationship where I wasn't appreciated—it was all too familiar.

Heal your childhood wounds. No matter how old you are, the inner child remains and the hurt remains until you address it, bleeding into your adult relationships.

Acknowledgment to My Mom

Thank you; you did the best you could. I credit you for who I am and I take pride in calling you, my mother. I am so honored to be your daughter. I wouldn't want it any other way. This is my story, and it wouldn't be this had things been different. So, thank you.

To My Ex

I am forever grateful for you; you too did the best you could with what you knew at the time. I know you didn't intentionally hurt me or do the things you did with malice. I know you were hurting and had a lot of healing to do from your childhood wounds. It was a battle that I couldn't fight for you, no matter how much I wanted to help. It hurt me to see you go down that path, but I know that this too is your story, and it allows you to grow and learn. They are all lessons that allow us to become the person we are meant to become. Thank you, as out of this through us—*Heaven on Earth* was birthed. This is exactly how everything was supposed to happen.

To My King

To my King, my Father, my Savior, my Healer, my Provider, my Creator...THANK YOU. Thank you for choosing me. Thank you for choosing me to fulfill this mission, this purpose to uplift, heal, and impact women in this way. Thank you once again for choosing me. The odds were against me, but YOU chose me. Heaven on earth...

About the Author

Irene Barrera is on a mission to help women heal from their past and live their lives in accordance with what the Lord has in store. She firmly believes that processing traumas from childhood and learning to trust in God are imperative to finding the freedom to live a deeply rewarding life without fear. Healing and forgiveness are integral in the process, but so is finding worth in Christ.

The author owns a successful fitness studio focused on women and is known for her inspiring spiritual retreats and speaking engagements. She immerses herself in seeking the Lord daily and finding ways to connect with Him as well as helping others to connect with and follow Him.

The Boston native enjoys the peace of the beach, the company of family, and the deep fulfillment of helping women find their true worth and healing through Christ so they can thrive in life.

About Serene Purpose

Serene Purpose
Boston, MA

Our mission is to support women's healing in all that which we create (books, retreats, etc); allowing them to feel empowered, while reaching a new level of serenity as they heal. Therefore creating a life filled with purpose.

There is a reason for your existence, for your pain, for the process, and that is your purpose. God's calling for your life.

If this book spoke to you, you may also want to check out our life changing retreats.

Website: www.heavenonearthbook.co

Instagram: @heavenonearthbook

Made in United States
North Haven, CT
06 May 2022